Everything You Need to Know About

Public Speaking

Actor and comedian Bill Cosby is a talented and entertaining public speaker.

Everything You Need to Know About

Public Speaking

Rachel Blumstein

The Rosen Publishing Group, Inc.
New York

Published in 2000 by The Rosen Publishing Group, Inc.
29 East 21st Street, New York, NY 10010

Copyright © 2000 by The Rosen Publishing Group, Inc.

First Edition

Library of Congress Cataloging-in-Publication Data

Blumstein, Rachel.
    Everything you need to know about public speaking / Rachel Blumstein.
        p. cm. -- (The need to know library)
    Includes bibliographical references and index.
    Summary: Describes public speaking skills with practical advice such as choosing a topic, writing a speech, using visuals, practicing, and conquering stage fright.
    ISBN 0-8239-3087-4
    1. Public Speaking—Juvenile literature. [1. Public speaking.] I. Title. II. Series.
PN4121 .B5275 2000
808.5'1—dc21

                                    99-055491

Manufactured in the United States of America

Contents

Introduction: "Why Do I
            Have to Give a Speech?"   6

Chapter One   Conquering Stage Fright   9

Chapter Two   Choosing and
               Brainstorming Your Topic 14

Chapter Three Outlining Your Speech   24

Chapter Four   Writing Your Speech   33

Chapter Five   Capturing Your Audience
               with Visuals   41

Chapter Six   Editing and Practicing
               Your Speech   48

Chapter Seven The Day of Your Speech   52

               Glossary   57

               Where to Go for Help   60

               For Further Reading   62

               Index   63

Introduction: "Why Do I Have to Give a Speech?"

If you are reading this book, chances are you did not volunteer to stand in front of a group of people and speak. Few people volunteer to walk over hot coals or roast slowly over an open fire—and most people fear public speaking more than physical pain or death. In fact, in a list of adults' top ten fears, death ranked #7, whereas fear of public speaking appeared as #1. Yet someone (probably an adult) has asked, cajoled, perhaps even *insisted* that you "say a few words" to your class, team, club, church, or synagogue. If adults fear public speaking so much, why do they ask you to do it?

This may be the first time you have to speak in public, but it certainly will not be the last. Throughout your life, even if you strive to avoid it, you will, inevitably, be required to speak in public. Some professions require speaking more than others do, but all jobs require communication skills. Ask some adults if they use public speaking skills in their profession, and you will find that almost everyone does—teachers, actors, doctors, salespeople, lawyers, engineers, politicians, musicians—whether they are speaking from a stage to a crowd of thousands or giving the occasional report at a staff meeting.

The world of work is not the only place you will be asked to give a speech. At your brother's wedding you may be expected to give a toast. You may want to educate your community board about the importance of recycling or convince the school board to raise teachers' salaries.

Booker T. Washington, born as a slave on a plantation in Virginia, grew to become one of the most important educators of his time. He valued public speaking so much that he devoted an entire chapter of his biography, *Up from Slavery,* to the topic. Washington established the Tuskegee Institute and became a consummate speaker who would fill halls with people who stood for hours to hear him intone on the importance of education for African Americans. After years of public speaking, one might assume that Washington overcame the natural fear of speaking before a crowd. Yet Washington wrote that he always suffered from nervousness before speaking. "More than once, just before I was to make an important address, this nervous strain

Booker T. Washington was a powerful public speaker.

has been so great that I have resolved never again to speak in public." Yet he did speak again and again because the importance of what he had to say outweighed his fears. Washington tells his readers, "It seems to me that there is rarely such a combination of mental and physical delight in any effort as that which comes to a public speaker when he feels that he has a great audience completely within his control." The ability to successfully express yourself is a door to power. In this book we will provide you with some keys to unlock that door.

Chapter One | Conquering Stage Fright

Moments before you are about to give a class presentation, your pulse quickens, your breathing becomes shallow, and you may experience muscle spasms in your voice box, knees, and hands; your hands feel cold, your palms feel sweaty, your mouth gets dry, and you may even feel nauseous. You are experiencing a fear of public speaking. In this chapter, you will learn some strategies to work through your fear and alleviate some of the symptoms.

First Things First

Step #1: Accept that you will never completely overcome the butterflies in your stomach that appear when you have to speak in public. However, these fears can be used to your advantage. As a presenter, you should concentrate on, in one instructor's words, "getting the butterflies to fly in formation." Imagine that you hold a coin in your hand. One side of the coin says "Fear," and the flip side says "Excitement." Many of the symptoms of fear are the same ones you experience when you fall in love or before you are about to compete in an important track race. You experience them because you want to succeed, and if you do not let the symptoms overwhelm you, you can use your fears to goad you on to success.

Step #2: "Break down" the audience. Reminding yourself that the audience is human, and not a monster, will make you feel more comfortable. Your audience probably consists of peers, such as your classmates, or your family and community. Most likely, they want you to succeed.

Stress Busters

Below are instructions for two different relaxation exercises, or "stress busters." Think of using these relaxation exercises to tame the butterflies. You may choose to use all of them, or only one, depending on what is most effective for you and how much time you can find to be alone before your speech. Try to find some time and a space where you can be alone to relax. For example, if it is a class presentation, you can try to take a few minutes in the restroom before class to work on one of the following exercises. If these exercises are impractical for you, use them as a springboard to develop your own.

Try to find some time and a space where you can be alone to relax before your speech.

Stress Buster #1

This common muscle relaxation technique involves tensing and then relaxing different muscle groups. Each muscle group should be tensed for ten seconds and allowed to relax for fifteen to twenty seconds. All of the other muscles in your body should remain relaxed as you concentrate on each muscle group. First, find a quiet, comfortable place.

1. Take three deep breaths. Concentrate on exhaling slowly. As you exhale, close your eyes and imagine your stress flowing out of you and then away from your body.

2. Clench your fists. Hold for ten seconds, then let go

suddenly. Concentrate on the feeling of limpness you experience for fifteen to twenty seconds.

3. Tense your biceps by "making a muscle" with each arm. Hold for ten seconds, then relax for fifteen to twenty seconds.

4. Tense your triceps, the muscles on the undersides of your upper arms, by extending your arms and holding them straight for ten to fifteen seconds.

5. Wrinkle your forehead by raising your eyebrows. Hold, and then relax.

6. Wrinkle up the muscles of your face. Hold your eyes tightly shut. Purse your lips, and hunch your shoulders. Hold and feel the tension. Release and feel the limpness.

7. Arch your back. Hold, and then release.

8. Tighten your chest muscles by taking a deep breath and holding the tension in. Release.

9. Tense your stomach muscles by holding your stomach in, then release.

10. Tighten your buttocks and thighs. Release.

11. Tense calves by flexing feet. Release.

12. Tighten feet by curling toes. Release.

13. Now take a moment to mentally scan your

body. If you continue to feel tension in a partic-ular area, repeat the exercise in that muscle area.

14. Feel relaxation flowing through your body, starting at the tip of your head, and gradually flowing through every muscle group in your body, down to your toes.

Stress Buster #2

Imaging, or visualization, is my personal favorite of the relaxation exercises. In this exercise, you visualize yourself succeeding. As in stress buster #1, find a com-fortable position and close your eyes. As if you are playing a video or movie in your head, imagine yourself standing in front of the group you are about to address. See yourself beginning your speech in front of a hushed room. The audience listens attentively as you speak clearly and slowly. As you wrap up your speech, you receive a rousing round of applause. There are a couple of questions from the audience and you answer them completely and expertly. Then you take your seat and sigh with relief. Bask in that feeling of relief, as you are about to embark on chapter 2, where you will take the first steps to preparing your speech.

Chapter Two

Choosing and Brainstorming Your Topic

The "soul," or substance, of your speech is founded on your topic. Unless you have been assigned a subject or something comes to mind immediately, choosing a topic is often one of the most difficult parts of public speaking. Peggy Noonan, a political speechwriter, says, "It is harder to decide what you want to say than it is to figure out how to say it." Even if you have been assigned a topic, you may find you have a degree of flexibility to choose what aspect of the subject to highlight. Following are some guidelines for choosing a topic:

Choose a Topic You Care About

When Mrs. Washington told her class they could speak about anything, nothing came to Ronnie's mind. When she complained to her family about her lack of ideas, Ronnie's uncle offered to help by telling her all about optometry, his profession. He would give her all of the information she needed for a speech on evaluating vision and fitting people for eyeglasses. It sounded perfect (and easy) to Ronnie. The only problem was that the more Uncle Pete talked about optometry, the less Ronnie cared about optometry. None of the information seemed to be sinking in. This topic bored Ronnie—and she wondered how it could possibly interest her classmates.

Interviewing relatives, neighbors, teachers, and friends about their professions or hobbies can create the foundation for a *fantastic* speech, if you care about their professions or hobbies. Ronnie's mistake was that she didn't bother to find out if she liked her topic before she committed to speaking on optometry. If you don't care about your topic, your audience will sense your lack of interest. And no one wants to listen to a speaker drone on about something they don't have an interest in. As Jamie Humes, author of *The Sir Winston Method*, said, "People don't care how much you know unless they know how much you care."

Put simply: If you don't care, change the topic. If you are not allowed to change your topic, ask your teacher or the person who assigned it to explain why this subject is important. Engaging them in your struggle may convince them to change the topic or may help you to find a side of the topic that interests you.

Choose One (and Only One) Topic

For her public speaking assignment in English class, Marie chose the topic "Politics in America Today." Marie began to research her speech. She tried to include an introduction to the three arms of government, as well as descriptions of the Democratic and Republican parties and something about President Clinton's possible impeachment. Soon she worried how she could fit all of this into a ten-minute speech. Marie found she barely had time to finish researching, let alone write the speech and practice it before her turn to speak before the class.

Marie had bitten off more than she could chew. Her speech was not one speech, but many. Topics such as "Politics in America" are immense. Not only was the subject difficult for Marie to get her hands around, but the class understood little of what Marie said because she crammed so many details in, spoke so quickly, and failed to sum up main points. A better topic would be "How Our Electoral System Works" or even a subject as small as "Senator Schumer's Views on the Environment." This brings us to our second rule of choosing your topic.

Interviewing relatives about their professions can create the foundation for a fantastic speech, if you care about their professions.

Pick One Manageable Topic to Talk About (and Stick to It)

Ruth still did not have a topic for the public speaking state championship competition and began to worry that she would let down her school's team.

"I'm sorry, Coach, I've been distracted because my grandmother just came to live with us. Her health's not so great right now . . . "

As Ruth's coach inquired about her grandmother, an idea came to Ruth.

"Hey Coach, I could talk about my grandmother's struggle with cancer."

17

Most well-loved novels are written about family stories, both real and imagined. A speech about your family or a personal achievement or experience can make for powerful speaking material because the audience will sense your personal commitment and trust you. However, you have to work hard to engage others in personal topics. For example, do not tell inside jokes that only your family would understand. *Do* try to make your story relate to others' experiences. For example, Ruth could describe her grandmother's illness and compare and contrast it with others' experiences.

Know Your Audience

During the preparation for his Bar Mitzvah, a Jewish celebration commemorating entrance into adulthood, David discovered, much to his dismay, that he would have to give a speech in front of his family, friends, and synagogue members during Saturday morning services.

"This is your speech, David, your moment to shine! What do you want to talk about?" asked the rabbi.

"I want to talk about baseball or cars . . . and tell South Park *jokes," David answered.*

"If you can relate baseball or cars to the Bible, and manage to leave time to thank your parents

When choosing a subject for a speech, such as the one you might have to give at your Bar Mitzvah, consider your audience, and speak about something that will interest them as well as you.

and the congregation, that's fine . . . but let's forget about the South Park *jokes, O.K.?* "

Choose a topic that is appropriate to the situation. Consider the age and the temperament of your audience, and speak about something they can understand and appreciate.

The Five Ws

O.K. So you have to come up with a speech about something you are interested in, stick to one topic, and make it something the audience can relate to and understand. Suddenly it seems you are not interested in anything. It's time to play reporter and interview yourself. Journalism students are taught to use the "five Ws" (*who, what, when, where,* and *why*) in researching news stories. The five Ws provide a brainstorming tool that you can use to come up with and investigate a topic. If you are having trouble developing a topic, try asking yourself these questions:

- Who am I? Who are the people that inspire me: family members, movie stars, baseball players, politicians, etc.?

- What do I love to do? What do I feel strongly about, either for or against? What can I do to change the world or my neighborhood?

- Where did I come from? Where is my family from? Where would I love to live? To travel?

- When do I feel inspiration?
- Why are we here?

Every Speech Has a Job

What is the purpose of your speech? Once you have chosen a topic, it is time to decide what type of speech you are writing. What is your speech designed to do? Speeches can do a number of things.

Speeches to Inform

You want to teach your audience new information or share an insight. However, you need to do more than just provide the facts—you also have to help your audience interpret them.

Examples of topics for informational speeches:

- "How to Train a Horse"
- "My Experiences with Glassblowing"
- "The Effects of Secondhand Tobacco Smoke"

Speeches to Motivate or Persuade

Motivational speeches rely on reasoning more than facts. Your goal is to convince the audience to accept a particular point of view—yours! Use a motivational speech to sell an idea to your audience, to change their minds, or to persuade them to take action.

21

It is important to know as much as possible about who your audience members are if you are going to persuade them. What are their beliefs? What is important to them? You need to tailor your speech so that it resonates with their experiences and desires. This is not to say that you have to tell your audience what they want to hear. Rather, a motivational speech should challenge them to think in new ways. For example, if you wanted to give your classmates a speech arguing for a school calendar that includes summers, you need to tell your peers what is in it for them—more vacations throughout the year, shorter school days, etc. If you were delivering a speech on the same topic to students' parents, your supporting points might be different. For example, you could emphasize the money parents will save on summer camps.

Examples of speeches to persuade:

- "Why We Need to Preserve Our Historical Buildings"

- "Putting the ADA into Action to Ensure That All Public Spaces Are Accessible to People with Disabilities"

- "Why Smoking Should be Outlawed—and What You Can Do About It"

You will notice that both example lists contain a speech about the ills of smoking. You could write an informational or a motivational speech about smoking. You could even give a humorous speech on smoking. You would do well to include personal experiences, facts, and figures in all types of speeches. As you develop your thesis in chapter 3, remember that what distinguishes informational and motivational speeches are their respective "jobs."

Chapter Three

Outlining Your Speech

Writing your speech begins with organizing your thoughts. And organizing your thoughts will not be overly difficult if you stick to the golden rule of public speaking developed by an old preacher who, when asked how he organized his sermons, answered: "I start by telling 'em what I'm going to tell 'em. Then I tell 'em. Then I tell 'em what I told 'em." The golden rule works because audiences best remember what was said first and last.

Brainstorming

When brainstorming, start with your own knowledge bank. Students hate to hear that they have been assigned a research project. The very word "research" seems to inspire fear. Before you run to the library to research your speech, ask yourself what you know about the topic. As mentioned in the last chapter, the best speeches focus on what the speaker is familiar with.

Return to journalism's five Ws (*who, what, where, when,* and *why)*, which we used in chapter 2 to find a topic. You can now use the five Ws to generate more thoughts on the content of your speech. Let's take the example of Joan, who was brainstorming for a speech about Princess Diana.

- Who: Princess Diana, member of the British royal family.

- What: Princess Di's charitable works; in particular, her work to rid the world of land mines (Joan realized she couldn't speak about the royal wedding, Di's death, and her charitable works all in one speech, so she chose to focus on one small topic).

- Where: In England; visits to third world countries.

- When: During her reign as princess (Joan was not sure how long Diana had campaigned against land mines—she had to do some research to find out).

- Why: Diana helped because she was a kind, generous person who had a sense of duty to help others in need.

After you have finished your investigation using the five Ws, you can continue the brainstorming process by freewriting. Simply write down everything that comes to mind when thinking about the topic. (You can also

One useful technique to use when brainstorming on a subject is to freewrite for a few minutes.

"freespeak" into a tape recorder and then transfer your ideas to paper later.) Don't worry about your style or editing your work. Remember that not all of what you write now will make it into your speech—just take this time to generate ideas. Also write down the questions that you will need to find answers to elsewhere—at the library or by interviewing family members or other kids.

For example, one question that Joan wrote down during her brainstorming process was, "Was Diana charitable even when she was a child?" Joan then wrote herself a note to go to the library and skim a biography of Diana for stories of her childhood that might answer this question. Even if you choose a topic that you know a lot about, you will still need to do some exploring or research to discover things you may not have known.

Your Thesis—the Bottom Line

"What's your speech about?"

Imagine that you have to come up with a clear and thorough one-sentence explanation to this question. That sentence is your thesis, your bottom line. After you have done a good chunk of brainstorming, you will be ready to develop your thesis. You want the audience to walk away with your main idea ringing in their ears. That main idea is the thesis.

Don't be afraid to let your thesis change as you research and write. You should, however, have a working thesis—a main idea to focus on as you develop your outline. After

Joan had answered the five Ws, she freewrote everything she knew about her topic and the questions she needed to research, and came up with the following working thesis: "Princess Diana was a unique role model who used her public position to achieve positive change in the world through her charitable work."

The Outline

Creating a speech without an outline is like exploring an unfamiliar city without a map. Use an outline to get organized, see the "lay of the land," note ideas you have left out and parts that can be put in the scrap heap. When you are creating your outline, you need only use short phrases and do not need to include details. The outline is a map designed to point you in the right direction, the foundation for your speech.

Your speech should have three basic sections, based on the preacher's golden rule:

- ◆ Tell 'em what you're going to tell 'em, or the introduction.

- ◆ Tell 'em, or the body.

- ◆ Tell 'em what you told 'em, or the conclusion.

Sound repetitive? It is, but with good reason. This repetition of main ideas will not only help to keep your audience focused, but it will keep you focused on the job of your speech: getting across your number one and only point, your bottom line.

An Outline of the Outline

When you have completed your outline, it should include these basic parts:

I. The Introduction

A. Grab the audience

B. Tell them what you're going to tell them

C. Tell the audience what's in it for them

II. The Body

A. Point #1

B. Point #2

C. Point #3

III. The Conclusion

The Introduction

As shown above, there should be three parts to your introduction:

- First, you have to win the audience's attention. You can do this by making a joke; using a prop; telling an anecdote, or brief story; asking a question; telling the audience a startling fact; or sharing a personal experience. Remember that these techniques are not limited to the introduction: You can use them to grab attention throughout your speech.

- Now that you have grabbed their attention, tell them what you have got in store for them. State your thesis, in no more than one or two sentences. At this point, you are merely introducing the audience to the idea that you are going to embellish in the body of the speech.

- What is in it for the audience? You need to tell them why they should listen to your speech; why they should care about what you have to say. To help you think of what your audience will get out of the speech, think about what interests you about the topic. Your audience may be interested in the same way. For example, you can say, "After you walk away from this speech, you will understand a few basic techniques of origami, or Japanese paper folding, and know where to go to learn more" or "At the close of my talk, I hope you will understand how second-hand smoke harms people and agree that it is time we make smoking a thing of the past."

The Body

This is the part where you "tell 'em." The body makes up the bulk of your speech. Try to organize the body of your speech into two to four points. Each point should be broad and include a piece of useful information, distinct from the other points, that supports your thesis. There are several ways to organize the body of your speech. You could try:

- Chronological order
- Cause and effect

◆ State the problem, then demonstrate the solution

The Conclusion

Time to wrap it up and "tell 'em what you told 'em." To bring your speech to a smooth conclusion, you can try one or more of the following:

- ◆ Tell the audience where they can find more information: "If you are interested in learning more about origami, I suggest reading *The Art of Origami.*"

- ◆ Tell them how they can make use of the information you have given them: "The information I have given you about how meat is processed should help you to make informed decisions about what to buy at the grocery store."

- ◆ Issue a challenge: "Now that you know about some of the effects of handgun accidents, and what steps we can take to prevent these accidents, I urge each of you to contact your representatives and tell them to support stronger gun control laws."

After you have developed your outline, look it over with a critical eye. Does it make sense? Does it say what you want to say? Did you leave out any key points? Are there parts that you can take out of your outline without losing part of your message? Take them out. Your outline is the skeleton of your speech, and it is now time to fill in the flesh and blood.

It is important for you to look over your outline with a critical eye.

Chapter Four

Writing Your Speech

Although this chapter is entitled "Writing Your Speech," you may decide not to "write" a speech at all. In fact, if you have thoroughly researched your topic and developed a solid outline, you may feel comfortable standing in front of an audience and using the outline to jog your memory as you talk about your topic. This method works particularly well if you know your topic inside and out, and feel comfortable with improvisation. At this point in the creation of your speech, you have a choice to make: You can keep your speech in outline form, or you can write it out word for word. There are pros and cons to each method.

Pros of working from an outline:

- Easier to maintain eye contact with audience
- Easier to "talk" to the audience rather than read to them (more about this in chapter 5)
- Less paper to shuffle

Cons:

- More likely to forget pieces of information
- Less security
- Need to spend extra time practicing

If you decide to write your speech word for word, think of it as a script that you are using for a performance.

Pros of using a script:

- Helpful in organizing thoughts
- If you forget parts, you have them in front of you
- You can remind yourself of stylistic issues (e.g., using a comma to remind yourself to breathe)

Cons:

- Harder to maintain personal contact with your audience
- More time consumed in writing

Write For the Ear

Whether you use an outline or a script, think of your speech as a performance and gear it toward the audience's ears. Remember that listeners are not able to go back and review what you have just said. That is why you have to "tell 'em what you told 'em." But you can also style your speech so that it is easier for listeners to attend to it. Style can liven up a speech.

Now it is time to flesh out the main points in the body of your outline, and add some pizzazz to your introduction and conclusion. As you develop your thesis, you can pepper your speech with grabbers and develop your own grammatical style. However, all of the pizzazz that you add to your speech should be centered on one goal: making your speech interesting and understandable to your audience. You may have fascinating, brilliant ideas to convey, but if your audience cannot understand them, your speech will not succeed. When writing your speech, you can make it clear by saying yes to short sentences, active verbs, and repetition of basic concepts; and by saying no to words that are hard to pronounce, sentences that do not flow easily, and long sentences, which make it hard to breathe.

Using Style in Your Speech

Style *n.* **1.** the manner of writing or speaking or doing something (contrasted with the subject matter or the

35

thing done). **2.** shape or design, *a new style of coat.* **3.** elegance, distinction.

The actress Audrey Hepburn had style. Peeking in the window of Tiffany's, delicately munching a croissant at 7 AM, wearing the perfect little black dress in the film *Breakfast at Tiffany's,* she expressed her distinct brand of style. The same can be said of Mia Hamm, a soccer superstar who is admired for her personal style of soccer playing as well as for the way she wears her hair. Personal style is a hard thing to pin down. Although both Audrey and Mia share the distinction of being performers, you would be hard-pressed to explain what else they have in common. Have you ever thought about your own personal style? You probably do consider it when you choose what clothes to wear. Now I will ask you to consider your personal writing and speaking style.

What is style in writing? The way you walk, what you choose to wear, how you speak—all of these factors contribute to your own personal style. They give others a window into who you are, your essence. Writing style is similar—the "clothes" that your speech "wears" and the way your speech "moves" are part of what draws listeners in. Great style cannot make up for the substance of the speech, but it can draw listeners in and keep their attention.

Whether you have decided to work from an outline or write out your script, you must keep style issues in mind.

Audrey Hepburn expressed her distinct brand of style in *Breakfast at Tiffany's*

Tricks of the Speech-Writing Trade

Be sure that number, tense, and gender match. Make smooth transitions from one idea to the next by using the following:

> To **add** an idea use *also, and, moreover, further, similarly.*

> To **compare** ideas use *in the same way, likewise.*

> To **contrast** ideas use *but, however, on the other hand, yet.*

> To show **cause and effec**t use *as a result, therefore, hence.*

You can use the following for dramatic effect in your speech:

> **Similes** use *as* or *like* to compare two things. Example: *He's as sweet as honey; she vanished like the snow..*

> **Metaphors** compare two things that are not literally alike without the use of *as* or *like*. Example: *You are the sunshine of my life; war is hell.*

> **Alliteration** uses the same sound or letter at the beginning of several words in succession. Example: *Sing a song of sixpence.*

> **Assonance** uses similar sounds between two syllables of successive words. Example: *The rain in Spain falls mainly on the plain.*

Repetition of the same words and/or ideas. Example: *"We demand health care for all, we demand better schools, we demand safer streets."*

Rhetorical Questions are phrased as questions for dramatic effect but do not demand an answer. Example: *"Would anybody like to learn how to make extra cash while sitting on the beach this summer?"*

Parallelism uses the repetition of similar phrasing for dramatic effect.
Examples: *"Ask not what your country can do for you; ask instead what you can do for your country"*; *"One small step for man, one giant leap for mankind"* ; *"It was the best of times, it was the worst of times."*

Final Thoughts on Writing Your Speech

Sticking to the outline in writing your speech will make it easy for the audience to follow. Do not let your train of thought be a mystery. For example, when you have reached the body of your speech, you can let the audience know that you have three main points to support your thesis. You can do this with phrases such as "My first point is"; "The second thing I want to tell you is"; "And, finally, the third thing you need to know is."

Fill in your outline by supporting your main points with stories, statistics, and facts. You can also use visual aids, discussed in detail in the next chapter. Make it personal. People want to hear what the topic means to you and to them. Additionally, people are usually more interested in hearing about people than hearing impressive statistics. If your speech is about earthquakes, you can include facts and figures, but a story (real or fictitious) about people who experienced an earthquake can make the topic come alive for your audience.

Chapter Five

Capturing Your Audience with Visuals

Forty-five percent of your message comes across through the words that you speak. But 55 percent of your message is conveyed through body language. That means that if your words are saying one thing and your body is saying another, the audience will believe what your body is saying.

But what is your body saying? How do bodies talk?

Consider the following scenario: You are watching a debate between two candidates for state senator. Each candidate speaks about his or her views on how public school education in your state can be improved. Candidate A is slumped in a chair, head down; his hands fidget with a piece of paper. He speaks so timidly that you can barely hear what he is saying. Candidate B

Bad posture and poor eye contact make it harder for your audience to follow what you are saying during your speech.

stands erect, faces her audience, looks you in the eye, gestures confidently with her hands, and speaks in a loud, clear voice. Before I even ask you who you would vote for, you are probably thinking, "C'mon, this isn't realistic—Candidate A would never even make it into the debate!" Body language speaks louder than words. It can mask your message, or it can help you to express yourself.

Your speech is a performance. Consider TV reporters as examples: Although they may have a script in front of them, they manage to look directly into the camera while speaking.

A famous sportscaster, Red Barber, said that when he read the news aloud to thousands of people over the television, he pretended that he was talking intimately to just one person. This helped him to maintain an intimate relationship with his audience.

With practice, you should be able to speak, rather than read, to the audience. If you find it difficult to maintain eye contact, try this method: Begin by looking down at your text or outline. Pick up the first part of the sentence you want to tell your audience, and look up at them to deliver that sentence. When you reach the end of a sentence or a pause, take that brief opportunity to look down at your script.

Visual Aids

Your audience will remember only 10 percent of what they hear. They will, however, retain 50 percent

Here are some pointers to help you express confidence and authority through body language:

- Have good posture, stand erect.

- Keep your chin up so that you are facing the audience.

- Do not be afraid to take up space. Stand with your legs slightly apart and balance your weight evenly on each foot. Keep your arms hanging loosely at your sides.

- Use gestures to "act out" your speech. Gestures can help the audience to understand.

- Maintain eye contact with all sections of the audience.

This brings us to the #1 rule to capturing your audience's attention: Do not read your speech. Rather, talk to your audience. This rule applies whether you have decided to go with an outline or use a script. If you read your speech you risk:

- Sounding monotonous and boring your audience

- Losing your place and stumbling

- Limited eye contact, which causes the audience to lose interest

Using physical gestures can help the audience to understand what you are saying.

of the information that they hear and see. Props and body language are important tools for capturing your audience's attention.

Examples of props include posterboard signs, pictures, or graphs; overheard projections; and flip charts. But you should also think creatively. For example, a student who gave a presentation on fly-fishing displayed a rod and some flies that he had made.

If you use visuals, choose your props wisely. The audience will pay attention to whatever you may be holding in your hand. Fiddling with a pen, for example, will distract the audience. Also, remember to keep it simple. If you use flip charts, overhead projections, or posterboard, make sure the information is large enough for everyone to see, is written clearly. Use simple sentences that everyone can quickly understand. Actively incorporate these visuals into your speech; do not merely hang up a poster and let it speak for itself. This will, again, distract people from what you are saying. Show the visual, explain it if necessary or merely refer to it, and then put it away.

If you use handouts, make sure they are distributed to your audience before you start speaking. If you distribute them during your speech, the audience will become distracted and focus on the handouts rather than your speech. Also, if you hand out materials, make sure to proofread them for spelling errors and inaccurate information.

Now you're ready to go . . . almost!

Props and body language are important tools for capturing your audience's attention.

Chapter Six | Editing and Practicing Your Speech

Now you have a finished product—your speech. But the truth is that your speech is not finished until you have rehearsed it. Practicing will help you to discover parts that work on paper but not in front of a crowd. One of the greatest benefits of practicing, however, is that it reduces nervousness. After you have practiced your speech several times, alone and in front of a "model audience," you know that you can do it. There is nothing like practice to boost your confidence.

Editing Strategies

Editing and practicing go hand in hand; as you edit, you are practicing, and as you practice, you find parts

Recording yourself reading your speech aloud and listening to it later can help you with editing and practicing your speech.

of your speech that need to be changed and improved.

There are some things you can do to make editing your speech a little easier. Be sure to read a double-spaced copy of your text or your outline, and make corrections and notes in the margins. It helps if you read your speech aloud to yourself. You may also want to tape-record it, and play the recording back to listen to yourself. Then, take a break from your speech. If you have allowed enough time to prepare, it is often useful to put down your speech, step back from it, and not look at it or think about it for a day or two. When you come back to it, you may have fresh ideas, or see things you need to change (or things you really like!).

Speed Limit

The cardinal sin of public speaking is the presenter's need for speed. People speak quickly because of nerves and because they "just want to get it over with." Yet speaking fast can cause the audience to miss out on your message.

How do you find the right pace? Try speaking at a speed that you think your audience will be able to keep up with. Then slow down that pace by about half.

Rehearsal Strategies

Begin by delivering your speech to yourself. If you feel comfortable, you can try presenting it to your image in the mirror. You may also want to videotape or audiotape yourself. People are often overly critical of their own appearance and voice. Keep in mind that your audience will probably be more forgiving than you are. Your speech is a performance. Even when you are rehearsing to yourself, refrain from reading your speech—perform it.

Practice your speech completely at least five or six times. You may want to focus on evaluating one aspect of your speech each time you practice. For example, during the first rehearsal you may focus on your flow of ideas, the second rehearsal on your gestures and body language, etc.

Gather together a "response group" of friends and family to serve as a practice audience. Your group ideally should include between three and five members to get a variety of responses. Ask everyone in your practice audience to come up with one positive aspect to praise in your speech, one question, and one suggestion for polishing the speech.

Every bit of practice contributes to your overall confidence about your speech!

Chapter Seven

The Day of Your Speech

Although there are certain things, such as pauses, breathing, and pitch of voice, that are very important, none of these can take the place of soul in an address.

—Booker T. Washington

Your big moment has arrived.

No sweat. You have chosen a topic that interests you and thought about how to make it come alive for your audience. You have researched. You have outlined and written an interesting speech—a speech full of style, a speech that is clear and thoughtful. You have rehearsed. You know what you want to tell your audience and you know how to say it. You are prepared.

Avoiding Pitfalls

The bad things you imagine happening probably won't. As Peggy Noonan says, " If they do, you'll survive . . . its only a speech." Below are some ideas to keep in mind before, during, and after your speech. Most important, do not get bogged down with checking equipment and choosing your outfit and forget the "soul" of your address. Keep believing in your message and that is what will come across.

Before Your Speech

- ◆ Dress for success. Wear clothes that are clean and comfortable. Looking good boosts confidence.

- ◆ Get to the venue early.

- ◆ Test your equipment.

- ◆ Check your props.

- ◆ Make sure your notecards or pages are in proper order.

- ◆ If you are nervous, try some of the relaxation exercises in chapter 1.

During Your Speech

- ◆ If you make a small mistake, such as mispronouncing a word, correct yourself but do not apologize. Apologizing draws attention to a mistake that the audience may hardly have noticed.

- Make eye contact with all sections of the audience, with the following exceptions: your friends and your enemies. A recent study shows that having familiar people in the audience who support you actually hurts your chances of successfully getting your point across. It seems we are distracted by the pressures of impressing our loved ones. If there are people in the audience who do *not* want you to succeed, do your best to ignore them. Pretend that they do not exist and focus on other audience members.

After Your Speech

After your speech, the audience may have questions. First repeat the question so that the rest of the audience can hear it. Answering questions can be tough when you have to think on your feet. Do not be afraid to say that you don't know the answer. The audience knows that you are being asked to give an impromptu response and will not judge you harshly for not having the correct answer. If you don't know the answer, tell them that you will find it out and get back to them, or let them know where they can go to find the answer.

A Final Thought: You Have Something to Say!

Do not be surprised if you find, after your speech is over, that you actually enjoyed the experience that

The audience may have questions about some of the issues you discussed in your speech.

ranks as adults' #1 fear. You may, in fact, decide to speak in public again because you have found that you have some important things to say.

A generation ago, children were taught to be seen and not heard. But voicelessness equals powerlessness. As you may have discovered from your first experience with public speaking, being able to express yourself produces a feeling of great accomplishment. There is strength in being able to show people how you think and feel. You have allowed an audience to understand a bit about your own experience of the world, and the audience will respect that experience. As a young adult, you deserve to be seen and heard, and others will benefit from hearing what you have to say.

Glossary

anecdote A short, amusing, or interesting story about a real person or event

brainstorm *n.* A sudden, bright idea. *v.* To engage in a conference designed to produce bright ideas.

cajole To coax.

cardinal Chief, most important.

chronological Arranged in the order in which things occurred.

consummate *v.* To accomplish, to make complete. *adj.* Supremely skilled.

convey To communicate as an idea or meaning.

demonstrate 1. To show evidence of, to prove. 2. To describe or explain with the help of examples. 3. To take part in a demonstration.

embellish   1. To ornament. 2. To improve (a story, etc.) by adding details that are entertaining but invented.

emphasis   1. Special importance given to something, prominence. 2. Vigor of expression or feeling or action.

feedback   Constructive criticism received from an audience about the strengths and weaknesses of a presentation, etc.

flexible   Adaptable, able to be changed to suit circumstances.

format   The shape and size of a book, speech, etc.

generate   To bring into existence, to produce.

gesture   An expressive movement of any part of the body.

grabber   Technique used to grab audience members' attention by surprising them or making them think.

improvise   1. To compose (a thing) impromptu. 2. To provide in times of need, using whatever materials are on hand.

incorporate   To include as a part.

informational speeches   Presentations used to teach an audience new material.

laliophobia   Fear of public speaking.

monotonous   Lacking in variety, tiring or boring because of this.

motivational speeches   Presentations used to motivate or persuade an audience to think or act.

optometry The profession of testing vision.

outline A sketch of the important sections of your speech, story, report, etc.

pizzazz Flamboyant elegance, vitality, zest.

proofread To read and correct.

script The text of a play or speech.

temperament A person's nature, as it controls how he or she behaves or thinks.

visual aids Props that help the audience to form mental pictures.

visualize To form a mental picture.

Where to Go for Help

Leaders of Tomorrow Foundation, Inc.
3919 East Laurel Lane
Phoenix, AZ 85028
Phone (602) 971-8944
Fax (602) 971-8955
E-mail: lot@treknet.net
Web site: www.speecheducation.com
Leaders of Tomorrow is dedicated to helping young people become better public speakers. It publishes What! I Have to Give a Speech? by Dr. Ken Snyder, as well as classroom materials and a video series. It also offers teacher training workshops.

Toastmasters International
P.O. Box 9052
Mission Viejo, CA 92690

(800) 993-7731 (9WE SPEAK)

Web site: www.toastmasters.org

Toastmasters is the largest non-profit public speaking organization. They provide workshops, conferences, and a variety of programs designed to help people develop public speaking skills. Contact them to learn about a group in your area.

For Further Reading

Drummond, Mary-Ellen. *Fearless and Flawless Public Speaking with Power, Polish, and Pizzazz.* Amsterdam: Pfeiffer & Company, 1993.

Noonan, Peggy. *On Speaking Well: How to Give a Speech with Style, Substance, and Clarity.* New York: ReaganBooks (an Imprint of Harper Perennial), 1998.

Otfinoski, Steven. *Speaking Up, Speaking Out: A Kid's Guide to Making Speeches, Oral Reports, and Conversation.* Brookfield, CT: Millbrook Press, 1996.

Vassallo, Wanda. *Speaking with Confidence: A Guide for Public Speakers.* Cincinnati: Betterway Books, 1990.

Washington, Booker T. *Up from Slavery.* New York: Random House/Modern Library, 1999.

Index

A

alliteration, 38
assonance, 38
audience, answering questions from, 13, 54
audience, capturing attention of, 29, 36, 44, 46
authority, 44

B

Barber, Red, 43
body language, 41–43, 46, 50
body of speech, 29, 30–31, 35
brainstorming, 20, 24–27
butterflies, 9–10

C

challenging the audience, 22, 31
clothes/dress, 36, 53
communication skills, 7
comparing ideas, 38
conclusion of speech, 29, 31–32, 35
confidence, 43, 44, 48, 51, 53
contrasting ideas, 38

E

editing, 27, 48–49
expressing yourself, 8, 43, 56
eye contact, 34, 43, 44, 54

F

facts, use of, 21, 23, 29, 40
familiarity with topic, 17–18, 25
fear, 6, 7, 9, 10, 24, 56
five Ws, 20–21, 25, 28

"freespeak," 27
freewriting, 25–26, 28

G

generating ideas, 25, 27
gestures, 43, 44, 50

H

handouts, 46
Humes, Jamie, 15

I

imaging/visualization, 13
improvisation, 33
informational speeches, 21, 23
introduction of speech, 29–30, 35

J

jokes/humor, 18–19, 23, 29

K

knowing your audience, 18–20, 22

M

metaphors, 38
mistakes, 53
model audience/response group, 48, 50–51
motivational speeches, 21–23

N

nervousness, 7, 48, 50
Noonan, Peggy, 14, 53

O

organizing, 24, 28, 30–31, 34
outline, 39, 43, 52
    creating/developing, 28–29, 32, 33, 40
    working from, 33, 34, 35, 36, 44

P

pace/speed of speech, 50
parallelism, 39
personal experiences, 23, 29
posture, 44
practicing/rehearsing, 34, 43, 48, 52
    strategies, 50–51
preparing/being prepared, 49, 52
props, 29, 46, 53

R

recording/taping of speech, 27, 49, 50
relaxation exercises, 10–13, 53
repetition, 28, 35, 39
research, 16, 20, 24, 25, 27, 28, 33, 52
rhetorical questions, 39

S

script, 34, 35, 36, 43, 44
similes, 38
speech as performance, 34, 35, 43, 50
statistics, use of, 40
style, 27, 34, 35–36, 52

T

thesis, 23, 27, 30, 31, 35, 39
topic, 14, 21, 22, 25, 28, 30, 33, 40
    choosing, 14–18, 20, 21, 27, 52
    developing, 20–21
transitions, 38
TV anchors, 43

V

visual aids, 40, 43–46

W

Washington, Booker T., 7–8, 52
working thesis, 28

About the Author

Rachel Blumstein has worked as an advocate for people with disabilities and their families. She is currently pursuing a Ph.D in School Psychology at New York University. She lives in Brooklyn, New York.

Photo Credits

Cover and pp. 11, 26, 42, 45, 47, 49, 55 by Kristen Artz; p. 8 © Archive Photos; p. 17 by Les Mills; pp. 19, 37 © Corbis; p.32 by Bob Van Lindt

Layout Design

Michael J. Caroleo